DINOSAUR
COLORING BOOK FOR KIDS

DINOSAUR COLORING BOOK FOR KIDS
by Zoey Bird

ISBN: 978-1989588420

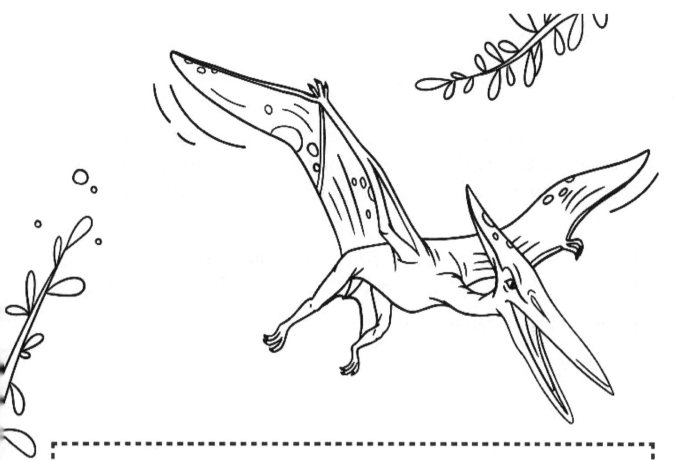

THIS BOOK BELONGS TO

_____

JOIN OUR FACEBOOK GROUP

In order to keep up with our latest and greatest kids activity and coloring books, I highly encourage you to join our warm community on Facebook. Here you will be able to connect to share games, fun activities, and books with others.

I am constantly adding tons of value. I'll update you on my latest books, and I'll even send free e-books that I think you'll find useful.

It would be great to connect with you there,

Zoey Bird

To Join, Visit: www.pristinepublish.com/activitygroup

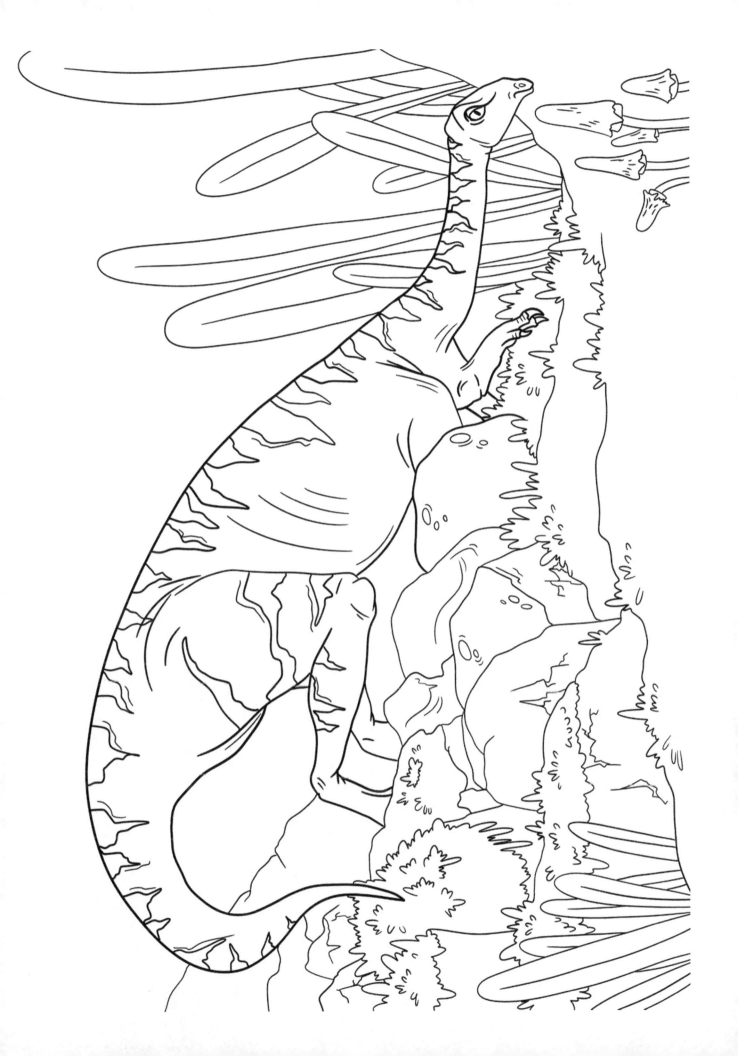

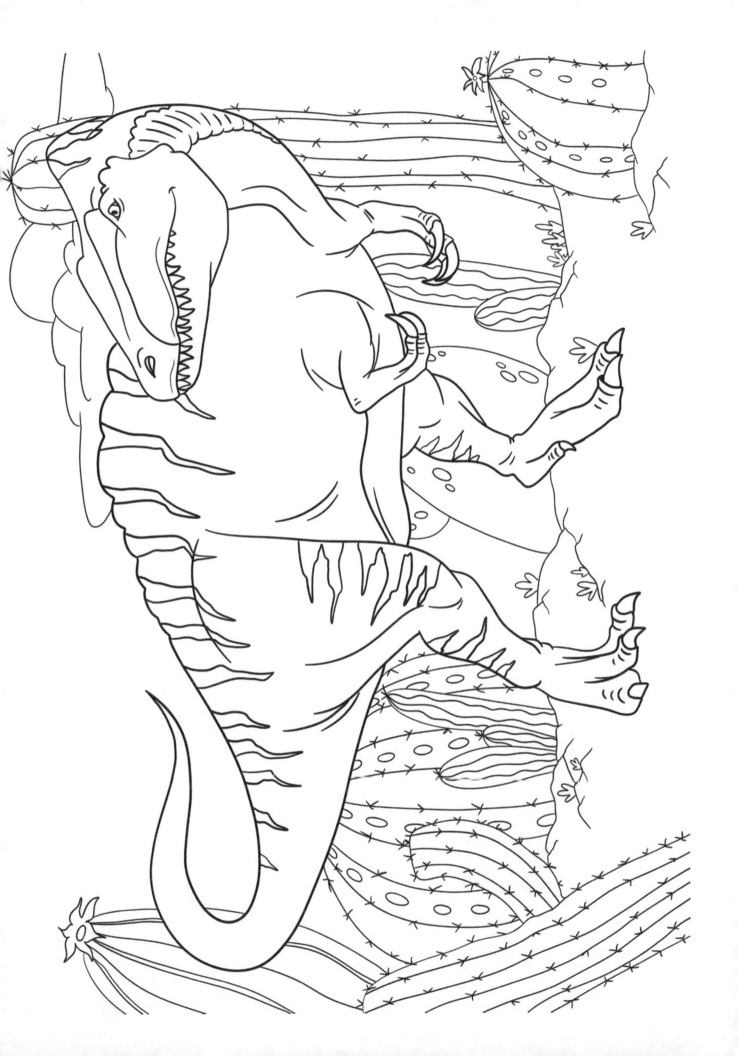

THANKS FOR COLORING!

I really hope you enjoyed this book, and most of all got more value from it than you had to give.

It would mean a lot to me if you left an Amazon review – I will reply to all questions asked!

Simply find this book on Amazon, scroll to the reviews section, and click "Write a customer review".

Or alternatively please visit www.pristinepublish.com/dinosaurreview to leave a review.

Be sure to check out my email list where I am constantly adding tons of value. The best way to currently get on the list is by visiting www.pristinepublish.com and entering your email.

Here I'll update you on my latest books, and I'll even send free e-books that I think you'll find useful.

Kindest regards,

CPSIA information can be obtained
at www.ICGtesting.com
Printed in the USA
LVHW101001050820
661945LV00042B/220

9 781989 588420